The Royal Horticultural Society

A Gardener's Five Year Record Book

FRANCES LINCOLN

Frances Lincoln Limited
4 Torriano Mews
Torriano Avenue
London NW5 2RZ

The Royal Horticultural Society
A Gardener's Five Year Record Book
Copyright © Frances Lincoln 2000

Text and illustrations copyright © The Royal
Horticultural Society 2000 and printed under
licence granted by The Royal Horticultural
Society, Registered Charity number 222879.

British Library cataloguing-in-publication data
A catalogue record for this book is
available from the British Library

ISBN 0-7112-1593-6

Printed in Hong Kong

First Frances Lincoln edition 2000

Front cover (clockwise, from bottom left): *Tulipa
schrenkii* x *T. stellata*; *T. clusiana* var. *chrysantha*
x *T. agenensis*; *T. praecox* x *T. clusiana* var.
chrysantha; *T.* 'Grose Goliath' (*T. stellata*
x *T. schrenkii*); *T. agenensis* x *T. clusiana* var.
chrysantha; *T. schrenkii* x *T. viridiflora*; and
T. praecox x *T. schrenkii*

Back cover: *Tulipa* 'General Ducksteyn'
(*T. clusiana* var. *chrysantha* x *praecox*)

Title page: *Sprekelia formosissima*

Right: *Paeonia officinalis* 'Rubra Plena'

The illustrations in this book have been taken from two of the many historic volumes of books and drawings donated to the Royal Horticultural Society's library by Reginald Cory, the Cardiff coal millionaire, in 1936.

The first is a florilegium drawn by Pieter van Kouwenhoorn, a painter who flourished in the 1620s and 1630s in Haarlem and Leiden in the Netherlands. His album originally contained 46 folios depicting some 200 different plants. Their names are given in Latin, French and German, but a few are left unnamed – perhaps due to van Kouwenhoorn's lack of familiarity with the plants. Drawn entirely from nature, the pictures include some of the popular flowers of the day, many of them comparatively recent introductions: fritillaries, hyacinths, irises, and above all, tulips.

Tulips also feature strongly in another volume featured in this book: an album of 33 coloured drawings from the early 18th century entitled *Hortus Florum Imaginum – A Garden of Flower Pictures*.

These drawings have been attributed to August Wilhelm Sievert, who was flower painter to the Duke of Baden and a teacher of the famous botanical artist Ehret. Some of the drawings were used as the originals for engravings in a celebrated German plant book, the *Hortus nitidissimis* (1750–93), edited by Christoph Jakob Trew.

We hope that you will enjoy making this beautiful book into a growing treasury of notes, observations, plans and reflections, and that it will be a valuable gardening assistant and companion over the next five years and beyond.

Brent Elliott
The Royal Horticultural Society

JANUARY

Leucojum vernum var. *carpathicum*

YEAR

YEAR

WEATHER

PLANTS
IN BLOOM

TASKS

NOTES

WEEK ONE

YEAR

YEAR

YEAR

WEEK TWO

YEAR

YEAR

WEATHER

PLANTS
IN BLOOM

TASKS

NOTES

Above: *Crocus* x *luteus*
Below: *Crocus vernus* ssp. *albiflorus*

WEEK TWO

YEAR

YEAR

YEAR

JANUARY

YEAR

YEAR

WEATHER

PLANTS
IN BLOOM

TASKS

NOTES

Crocus sativus

WEEK THREE

YEAR

YEAR

YEAR

WEEK FOUR

WEATHER

PLANTS
IN BLOOM

TASKS

NOTES

Above: *Crocus flavus*
Below: *Crocus sativus*

YEAR

YEAR

WEEK FOUR

YEAR

YEAR

YEAR

FEBRUARY

YEAR

YEAR

WEATHER

PLANTS
IN BLOOM

TASKS

NOTES

Fritillaria meleagris

FEBRUARY

WEEK ONE

YEAR

YEAR

YEAR

WEEK TWO

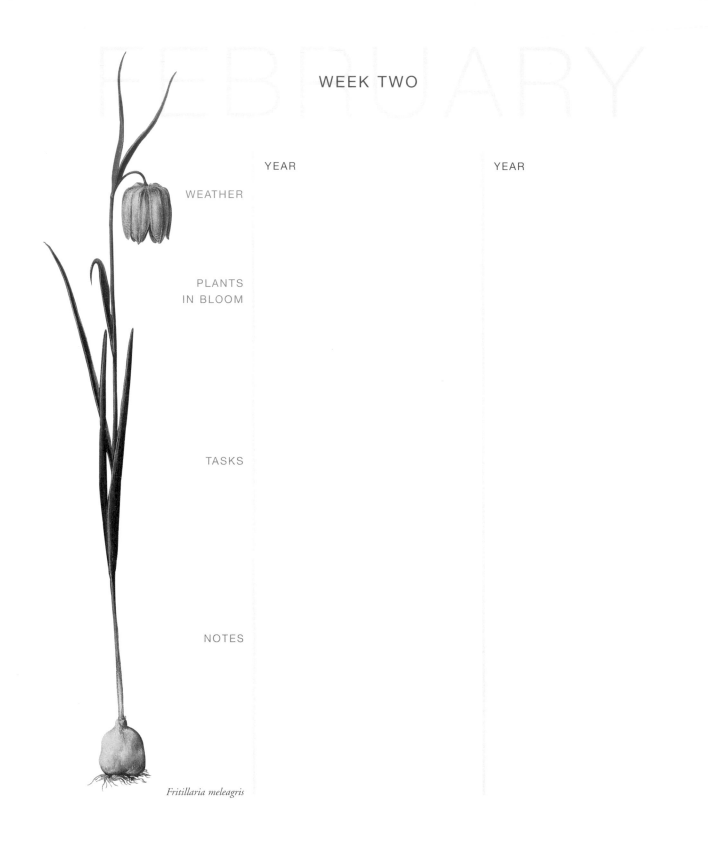

YEAR

YEAR

WEATHER

PLANTS
IN BLOOM

TASKS

NOTES

Fritillaria meleagris

WEEK TWO

YEAR

YEAR

YEAR

Narcissus 'Telemonius Plenus'

WEATHER

PLANTS IN BLOOM

TASKS

NOTES

YEAR

YEAR

WEEK THREE

YEAR

YEAR

YEAR

WEEK FOUR

YEAR

YEAR

WEATHER

PLANTS IN BLOOM

TASKS

NOTES

Narcissus hispanicus

WEEK FOUR

YEAR

YEAR

YEAR

MARCH

YEAR

YEAR

WEATHER

PLANTS
IN BLOOM

TASKS

NOTES

A polyanthus daffodil

WEEK ONE

YEAR

YEAR

YEAR

WEEK TWO

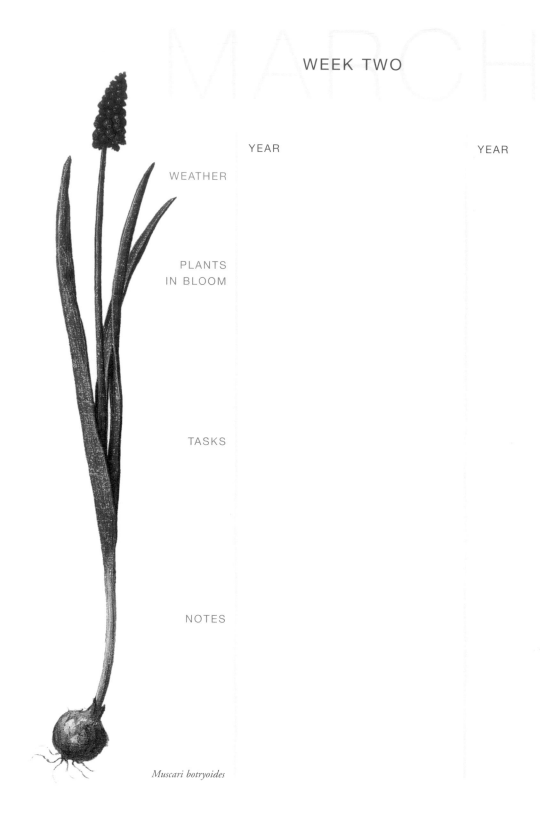

YEAR

YEAR

WEATHER

PLANTS
IN BLOOM

TASKS

NOTES

Muscari botryoides

WEEK TWO

YEAR

YEAR

YEAR

WEEK THREE

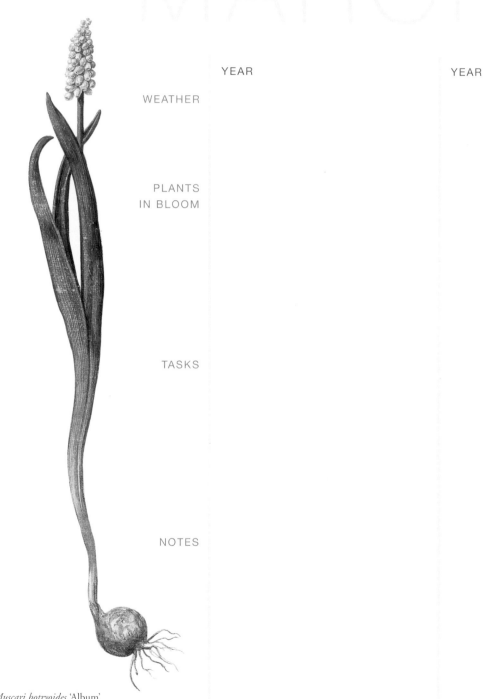

YEAR   YEAR

WEATHER

PLANTS
IN BLOOM

TASKS

NOTES

Muscari botryoides 'Album'

WEEK THREE

YEAR

YEAR

YEAR

WEEK FOUR

Hyacinthoides hispanica

YEAR

YEAR

WEATHER

PLANTS
IN BLOOM

TASKS

NOTES

WEEK FOUR

YEAR

YEAR

YEAR

APRIL

YEAR   YEAR

WEATHER

PLANTS
IN BLOOM

TASKS

NOTES

Hyacinthoides hispanica

WEEK ONE

YEAR

YEAR

YEAR

WEEK TWO

Brimeura amethystina

YEAR

YEAR

WEATHER

PLANTS
IN BLOOM

TASKS

NOTES

WEEK TWO

YEAR

YEAR

YEAR

APRIL

YEAR

YEAR

WEATHER

PLANTS
IN BLOOM

TASKS

NOTES

Spring-flowering
anemones

WEEK THREE

APRIL

YEAR

YEAR

YEAR

WEEK FOUR

YEAR 2003

YEAR 2003

WEATHER

Chilly. Changeable.

PLANTS
IN BLOOM

Ceanothus, Tulips
Fern fronds coming
Viburnum coming

TASKS

Rennig, Clear Compost
Grass.

NOTES

Used Nemashigan
Hostas and other
Slug nibbled!
Nema products for
Greenfly. etc.

Spring-flowering
anemones

WEEK FOUR

YEAR

YEAR

YEAR

MAY

WEATHER

YEAR   YEAR

PLANTS
IN BLOOM

TASKS

NOTES

Spring-flowering anemones

WEEK ONE

MAY

YEAR

YEAR

YEAR

WEEK TWO

Cultivated varieties
of anemones

YEAR

YEAR

WEATHER

PLANTS IN BLOOM

TASKS

NOTES

WEEK TWO

MAY

YEAR

YEAR

YEAR

WEEK THREE

YEAR

YEAR

WEATHER

PLANTS
IN BLOOM

TASKS

NOTES

Above: *Tulipa*
'Brandenburger'
(*T. clusiana* x *T. agenensis*)
Below: *Tulipa agenensis* x *T. viridiflora*

WEEK THREE

MAY

YEAR

YEAR

YEAR

WEEK FOUR

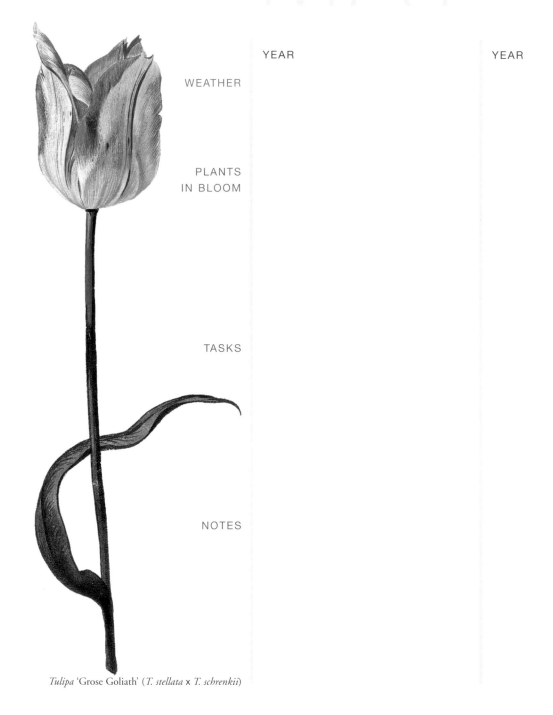

YEAR

YEAR

WEATHER

PLANTS
IN BLOOM

TASKS

NOTES

Tulipa 'Grose Goliath' (*T. stellata* x *T. schrenkii*)

WEEK FOUR

YEAR

YEAR

YEAR

JUNE

YEAR   YEAR

WEATHER

PLANTS
IN BLOOM

TASKS

NOTES

Tulipa 'General Ducksteyn'

JUNE

WEEK ONE

YEAR

YEAR

YEAR

WEEK TWO

YEAR   YEAR

WEATHER

PLANTS
IN BLOOM

TASKS

NOTES

Above: *Tulipa schrenkii* x *T. clusiana*
Below: *Tulipa clusiana* x *T. schrenkii* 'Semiplena'

WEEK TWO

YEAR

YEAR

YEAR

JUNE

Tulipa schrenkii x *T. clusiana*

YEAR

YEAR

WEATHER

PLANTS
IN BLOOM

TASKS

NOTES

WEEK THREE

YEAR

YEAR

YEAR

WEEK FOUR

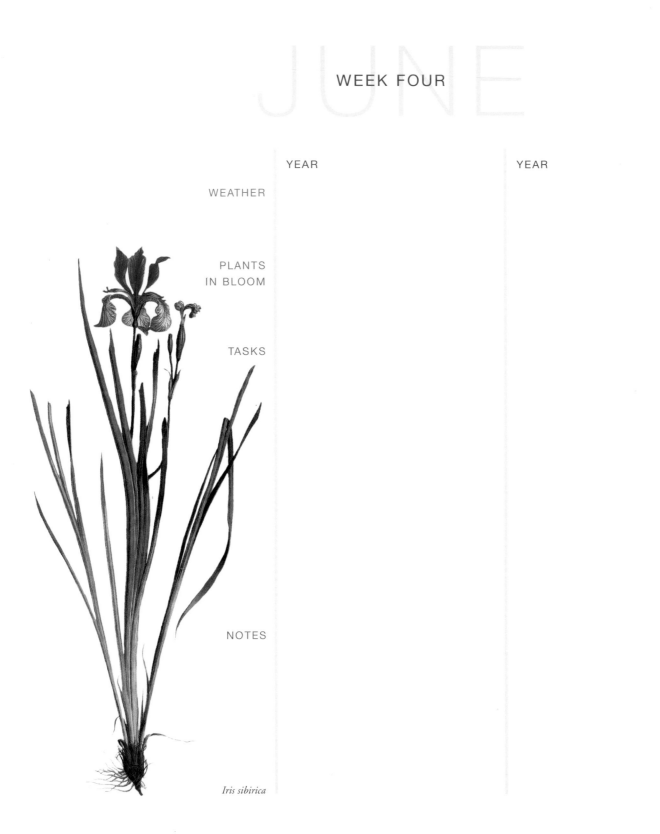

YEAR

YEAR

WEATHER

PLANTS
IN BLOOM

TASKS

NOTES

Iris sibirica

JUNE

WEEK FOUR

YEAR

YEAR

YEAR

JULY

YEAR   YEAR

WEATHER

PLANTS IN BLOOM

TASKS

NOTES

Iris xiphium

JULY

WEEK ONE

YEAR

YEAR

YEAR

WEEK TWO

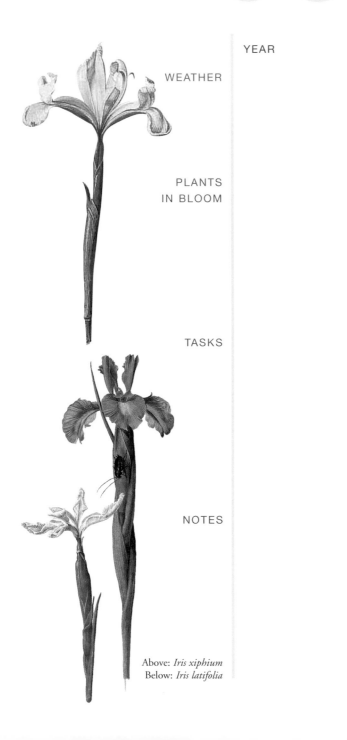

YEAR

YEAR

WEATHER

PLANTS
IN BLOOM

TASKS

NOTES

Above: *Iris xiphium*
Below: *Iris latifolia*

JULY

WEEK TWO

YEAR

YEAR

YEAR

WEEK THREE

Variants of
Aquilegia vulgaris

YEAR

YEAR

WEATHER

PLANTS
IN BLOOM

TASKS

NOTES

WEEK THREE

JULY

YEAR

YEAR

YEAR

WEEK FOUR

WEATHER

PLANTS IN BLOOM

TASKS

NOTES

Variants of *Aquilegia vulgaris*

YEAR

YEAR

JULY

WEEK FOUR

YEAR

YEAR

YEAR

AUGUST

YEAR

YEAR

WEATHER

PLANTS IN BLOOM

TASKS

NOTES

Variants of *Aquilegia vulgaris*

WEEK ONE

YEAR

YEAR

YEAR

YEAR

YEAR

WEATHER

PLANTS IN BLOOM

TASKS

NOTES

Adonis aestivalis

AUGUST

WEEK TWO

YEAR

YEAR

YEAR

WEEK THREE

YEAR

YEAR

WEATHER

PLANTS
IN BLOOM

TASKS

NOTES

Lychnis chalcedonica 'Alba'

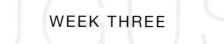

WEEK THREE

YEAR

YEAR

YEAR

AUGUST

WEEK FOUR

YEAR

YEAR

WEATHER

PLANTS
IN BLOOM

TASKS

NOTES

Lychnis chalcedonica

WEEK FOUR

YEAR

YEAR

YEAR

SEPTEMBER

Caltha palustris

YEAR

YEAR

WEATHER

PLANTS
IN BLOOM

TASKS

NOTES

WEEK ONE

SEPTEMBER

YEAR

YEAR

YEAR

WEEK TWO

YEAR

YEAR

WEATHER

PLANTS
IN BLOOM

TASKS

NOTES

Ranunculus acris 'Flore Pleno'

WEEK TWO

YEAR

YEAR

YEAR

WEEK THREE

YEAR

YEAR

WEATHER

PLANTS IN BLOOM

TASKS

NOTES

Ranunculus asiaticus

WEEK THREE

YEAR

YEAR

YEAR

WEEK FOUR

YEAR

YEAR

WEATHER

PLANTS
IN BLOOM

TASKS

NOTES

Dianthus caryophyllus

WEEK FOUR

YEAR

YEAR

YEAR

OCTOBER

YEAR   YEAR

WEATHER

PLANTS IN BLOOM

TASKS

NOTES

Saponaria officinalis 'Rosa Plena'

OCTOBER

WEEK ONE

YEAR

YEAR

YEAR

OCTOBER

WEEK TWO

WEATHER

PLANTS
IN BLOOM

TASKS

NOTES

YEAR

YEAR

Gladiolus italicus

WEEK TWO

YEAR

YEAR

YEAR

WEEK THREE

YEAR

YEAR

WEATHER

PLANTS
IN BLOOM

TASKS

NOTES

Hemerocallis lilioasphodelus

OCTOBER

WEEK THREE

YEAR

YEAR

YEAR

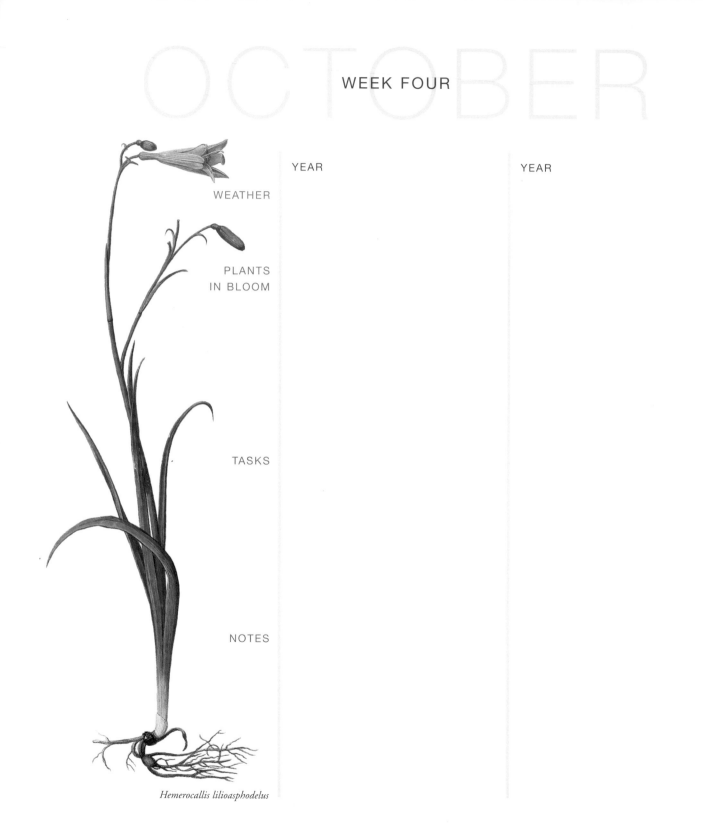

WEEK FOUR

WEATHER

PLANTS
IN BLOOM

TASKS

NOTES

YEAR

YEAR

Hemerocallis lilioasphodelus

OCTOBER

WEEK FOUR

YEAR

YEAR

YEAR

NOVEMBER

WEATHER

PLANTS
IN BLOOM

TASKS

NOTES

YEAR

YEAR

Lilium chalcedonicum

NOVEMBER

WEEK ONE

YEAR

YEAR

YEAR

WEEK TWO

YEAR

YEAR

WEATHER

PLANTS
IN BLOOM

TASKS

NOTES

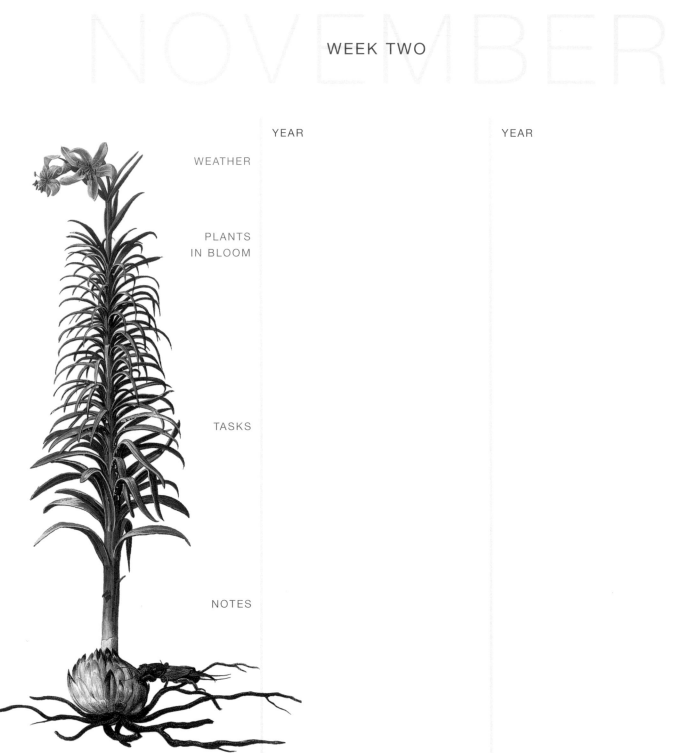

Lilium pyrenaicum

NOVEMBER

WEEK TWO

YEAR

YEAR

YEAR

WEEK THREE

YEAR

YEAR

WEATHER

PLANTS
IN BLOOM

TASKS

NOTES

Lilium martagon

WEEK THREE

YEAR

YEAR

YEAR

WEEK FOUR

YEAR

YEAR

WEATHER

PLANTS IN BLOOM

TASKS

NOTES

Gentiana acaulis

NOVEMBER

WEEK FOUR

YEAR

YEAR

YEAR

DECEMBER

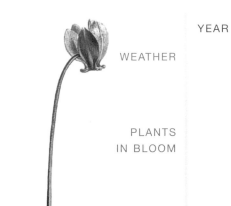

YEAR

YEAR

WEATHER

PLANTS
IN BLOOM

TASKS

NOTES

Above: *Cyclamen hederifolium*
Below: *Cyclamen repandum* 'Album'

DECEMBER

WEEK ONE

YEAR

YEAR

YEAR

WEEK TWO

YEAR

YEAR

WEATHER

PLANTS
IN BLOOM

TASKS

NOTES

Above: *Helleborus viridis*
Below: *Helleborus niger*

DECEMBER

WEEK TWO

YEAR

YEAR

YEAR

WEEK THREE

Eranthis hyemalis

YEAR

YEAR

WEATHER

PLANTS
IN BLOOM

TASKS

NOTES

DECEMBER

WEEK THREE

YEAR

YEAR

YEAR

WEEK FOUR

YEAR

YEAR

WEATHER

PLANTS IN BLOOM

TASKS

NOTES

Leucojum vernum var. *carpathicum*

DECEMBER

WEEK FOUR

YEAR

YEAR

YEAR

PLANTS TO BUY

PLANT NAME	WHERE SEEN	SUPPLIER	PLANTING POSITION

PLANTS TO BUY

PLANT NAME	WHERE SEEN	SUPPLIER	PLANTING POSITION

PLANT NAME	WHERE SEEN	SUPPLIER	PLANTING POSITION

PLANTS TO BUY

PLANT NAME	WHERE SEEN	SUPPLIER	PLANTING POSITION

PLANT SUPPLIERS

NAME	ADDRESS	TEL/FAX/E-MAIL

PLANT SUPPLIERS

NAME	ADDRESS	TEL/FAX/E-MAIL

PLANT SUPPLIERS

NAME	ADDRESS	TEL/FAX/E-MAIL

USEFUL ADDRESSES

NAME	ADDRESS	TEL/FAX/E-MAIL

GARDEN	WHEN TO VISIT	LOOK FOR

GARDEN	WHEN TO VISIT	LOOK FOR

GARDEN	DATE	COMMENT

GARDENS VISITED

GARDEN	DATE	COMMENT

NOTES